Rhyme Stones

Pat Skene
Illustrated by Graham Ross

ORCA BOOK PUBLISHERS

For Bruce, Estelle and Maureen—with love.

Text copyright © 2007 Pat Skene
Illustrations copyright © 2007 Graham Ross

Library and Archives Canada Cataloguing in Publication

Skene, Pat, 1945-
Rhyme stones / written by Pat Skene; illustrated by Graham Ross.

(Orca echoes)
ISBN 978-1-55143-636-4

1. Children's poetry, Canadian (English). I. Ross, Graham, 1962-
II. Title. III. Series.

PS8637.K46R49 2007   jC811'.6   C2007-903956-1

First published in the United States, 2007
Library of Congress Control Number: 2007930911

Summary: This mixture of long poems, short poems, interviews and collections of facts is
funny, engaging and informative: something for everyone.

Orca Book Publishers gratefully acknowledges the support for its publishing programs
provided by the following agencies: the Government of Canada through the Book
Publishing Industry Development Program and the Canada Council for the Arts, and the
Province of British Columbia through the BC Arts Council
and the Book Publishing Tax Credit.

Typesetting by Teresa Bubela
Cover artwork and interior illustrations by Graham Ross
Author photo by Cindy Taylor

Orca Book Publishers	Orca Book Publishers
PO Box 5626, Stn. B	PO Box 468
Victoria, BC Canada	Custer, WA USA
V8R 6S4	98240-0468

www.orcabook.com
Printed and bound in Canada.
Printed on 100% PCW recycled paper.

010 09 08 07 • 4 3 2 1

Contents

Cecil Goes Spelunking

There once was a boy who was scared of the dark.
"Oh, poor Cecil Bunker," his friends would remark.
They knew that he slept with a flashlight turned on.
He watched out for monsters all night until dawn.

Now Cecil's new puppy slept with him in bed.
"Don't worry, I'll save you, Fitzhugh," Cecil said.
When morning came Cecil would pick up his light.
It stayed in his pocket all day until night.

One late afternoon he met Wally and Will.
"Let's build a new fort," they said, "up on the hill."
So off through the forest they ran with Fitzhugh.
The boys were excited to build something new.

Then all of a sudden the pup disappeared.
"We'll help you to find him," his friends volunteered.
They checked under bushes and looked under rocks.
"That's him!" Wally hollered, but it was a fox.

"Let's hurry," said Cecil, "before it gets dark!"
And just at that moment, they heard a dog bark.
"That's got to be him," Will and Wally cried out.
"Fitzhugh…Fitzhugh…," Cecil started to shout.

The dog began howling which gave them a chill.
The boys listened closely and stood very still.
Then Cecil called out, "It's okay, boy, I'm here!"
He wondered how Fitzhugh could just disappear.

They scrambled through branches and followed the sound.
Then Will said, "It's coming from under that mound."
And that's when they saw it—a dark open hollow.
They stopped in their tracks and took a big swallow.

"A cave," Wally whispered. "We can't go in there."
And Will said, "It could be a den for a bear."
They heard Fitzhugh howling from somewhere inside.
And Cecil was tempted to run off and hide.

The call of his puppy was hard to ignore.
He hated the dark, but he loved Fitzhugh more.
Then with a deep breath, Cecil tried to be brave.
He flicked on his flashlight and entered the cave.

His friends watched him go with their eyes open wide.
"Just yell if you need us. We'll be right outside."
As Cecil went in he called, "Fitzhugh, I'm here."
The dog barked, and Cecil could tell he was near.

Then deep in the cave Cecil tripped and fell down.
His flashlight went out as it bounced on the ground.
He crawled in the dark of that black hollow space.
And Cecil thought, Monsters must live in this place.

When Fitzhugh stopped barking the cave was so still.
And Cecil heard nothing but silence until…
A flapping of wings made a *whoosh* in the air.
Now Cecil was sure there was something in there.

He felt his heart quicken. He felt his knees shake.
He said, "If I'm dreaming, please pinch me awake."
The blackness around him was velvety thick.
Poor Cecil was sure he was going to be sick.

He crept through the darkness and searched for his light.
Above, he imagined cave-monsters in flight.
And just when he thought he could take it no more…
He touched something cold on the muddy cave floor.

"My flashlight!" he cried out and clicked the switch on.
He hoped that the wing-flapping-monsters were gone.
The beam of his flashlight shone bright on Fitzhugh.
Now Cecil stood frozen, not sure what to do.

The dog was just sitting—surrounded by bats!
The two on his head flopped like raggedy hats.
And hundreds of bats hung in clumps upside-down.
"I'll save you," cried Cecil. "I won't let you down."

The cave full of bats had made Cecil turn pale.
But Fitzhugh the puppy was wagging his tail.
He looked quite content as he licked his new chums.
And Cecil thought, This is as strange as it comes.

"Just look at you!" Cecil cried out with a grin.
"You must have been howling to make me come in.
I thought you were trapped or in trouble," he said.
"And here you are sitting with bats on your head!"

Now Cecil was pleased he had no one to save.
So he used his flashlight to check out the cave.
The walls seemed to sparkle with crystals and gems
and coral-like flowers with curlicue stems.

He beamed his light up—the stalactites hung down,
like icicles dusted in cinnamon brown.
They clung to the ceiling and reached for the ground,
while some looked like soda-straws, hollow and round.

And then Cecil Bunker went on to explore.
Around him, stalagmites grew up from the floor.
He saw shapes like broomsticks and pancakes in stacks.
Weird corkscrew formations were clustered in packs.

It's awesome, he thought. What a beautiful sight.
I'm seeing the dark in a whole different light.
"Let's go now. It's time to go home," Cecil said.
And off flew the bats to their roost overhead.

So Fitzhugh and Cecil walked out of the cave.
And Wally and Will said they thought he was brave.
The boys were relieved that their friend was okay.
They carried him round on their shoulders all day.

And never again did he sleep with his light.
Or wait up for monsters to come out at night.
He conquered the darkness just like a spelunker.
And now all the kids call him "Brave Cecil Bunker."

An Interview
with Cecil Bunker

1. What is a spelunker?

Cecil: A spelunker is a person who explores caves. That's what I did to find Fitzhugh. But going into a wild cave in the woods like I did isn't always a good idea. There could be lots of danger inside, like falling rocks, water, animals and snakes. I'm glad Fitzhugh picked a good cave for spelunking.

2. What is a "wild cave"?

Cecil: Caves that have not been developed by humans are "wild caves." That's why they can be dangerous for kids. But "show caves" are safe and fun to explore. They have lights inside and tour guides to show you around. Some show caves have bridges, boats, waterfalls and awesome formations.

3. Do bats try to get in your hair?

Cecil: That's an old made-up story. Bats don't want to live in your hair. They look for shadowy places to roost, like in caves, under bridges, in trees and places like attics. Did you know that bats have four fingers and a thumb like people? Some bats carry rabies which could make you very sick. So it's best to stay away from bats.

4. Are there different kinds of bats?

Cecil: There are nearly one thousand different kinds of bats. And yes, there are vampire bats, but they don't turn into Count Dracula at night. Lots of bats eat only fruit and insects. In fact, in one night alone, three hundred bats can eat almost one million mosquitoes. Yummy!

5. How big are bats?

Cecil: They come in all sizes. The bats in my cave were small like birds. The tiny bumblebee bat is the size of a jellybean. But the flying fox bat has the wingspan of an average man with his arms stretched out. Pretty cool! I'm glad there wasn't a colony of flying fox bats in my cave.

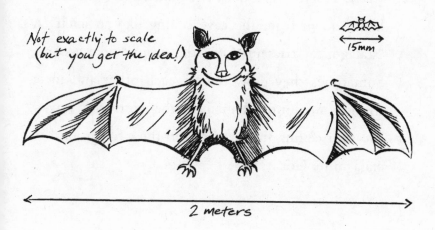

Not exactly to scale (but you get the idea!)

15mm

2 meters

6. Do bats have feathers like birds?

Cecil: Bats aren't birds—they're mammals like we are. They're warm-blooded and have fur. Bat wings are made of two thin layers of skin stretched over their arms and fingers. And bat babies are called pups, just like Fitzhugh.

7. What's the difference between a "stalactite" and a "stalagmite"?

Cecil: Everyone gets these two mixed up. A "stalactite" hangs down from the cave ceiling like an icicle. A "stalagmite" rises up from the ground like a cone. Sometimes they grow toward each other and meet to form a column. Remember the words this way— the *c* for ceiling in stala*c*tite and the *g* for ground in stala*g*mite. Got it?

8. How are cave formations made?

Cecil: They start with a single drop of water that seeps through the cracks of the cave. The water drips and leaves small calcium deposits on the floor, ceiling and walls of the cave. It can take nearly 150 years for 1 inch (or 2.5 centimeters) of stalactite to form. Imagine that.

9. Do cave formations really sparkle in the light?

Cecil: Most of them do because there are lots of dissolved minerals in the formations. When you shine a light on the different shapes, they reflect a rainbow of colors. The inside of many caves sparkles like a magic wonderland.

10. Can you take stuff from the cave as souvenirs?

Cecil: Oh, no. It's important not to touch any of the delicate formations in a cave. They're very fragile, and some have taken thousands of years to form. But if you go, take your camera. You can bring home lots of picture souvenirs. Happy spelunking!

Polly Palooka

Now Polly is being a bully again.
She's picking on me and last week it was Jen.
    I'm not going to cry.
    I'll hold my head high.
And tuck in my temper by counting to ten.

She teases and taunts us and breaks every rule.
My stomach hurts thinking about her at school.
    One day she kicked Mike.
    She broke Sarah's bike.
I guess Polly thinks being nasty is cool.

My friends say to punch her, but I don't agree.

'Cause using my fists to fight back isn't me.

    I tried to be nice.

    I smiled at her twice.

But Polly Palooka's still mean as can be.

I talk to my school friends when I get upset.
And Polly does things that are hard to forget.

She laughs at my clothes.

She pinches my nose.
Then Polly looks gladder the madder I get.

I wonder why Polly behaves in this way.
And why does she think hurting kids is okay?

She acts like hot stuff.

Well, I've had enough!
I'm tired of feeling so scared every day.

So I told my parents and teachers the facts.
I asked them to help us stop Polly's attacks.

Now we walk away.

Ignore her each day.
And when Polly bullies us, no one reacts.

The Bully Bulletin

Polly Palooka is a bully. And bullying is a big deal! It's a problem that affects lots of kids every day. Here are some things you can do when you meet a bully.

1. Keep your cool.

Getting angry won't solve the problem. It could even make things worse. Bullies love it when you get upset. It makes them feel more powerful. A bully doesn't care that you feel bad. In fact, the sadder and madder you get—the happier they are. Don't give bullies the satisfaction.

2. Don't bully back.

Fighting is against the rules in and out of school. Sometimes you might have to defend yourself. But getting into a scrap with a bully could get you hurt or in trouble. Real life isn't like television and video games. Fighting breaks bones and doesn't solve anything.

3. Put bullies on ignore.

Bullies love attention and live for your reaction. The best thing you can do is act brave and walk away—every time. When you ignore bullies, it sends a message that you don't care. Then you rob them of their bullying thrill. Soon, they'll probably get bored and leave you alone.

4. Talk about it.

Tell an adult about the problem. That's one of the most important things you can do. Parents, teachers and your friends can all help you to stop the bully. Don't suffer in silence. Talk it out with people who care about you.

5. Buddy-up.

Walk with friends to and from school. Stay in groups at recess, on the bus or wherever you might meet the bully. Don't walk away if someone else is being bullied. Kids can support each other by sticking together. Let the bully know that treating people that way isn't okay. Bullies aren't cool. No one likes a bully!

Halloween For Ernestine

It happened every Halloween—
a little witch called Ernestine
was so afraid of being seen
because she couldn't fly.
She tried to fly.
Could she be shy?

She sneaked about her witch's lair,
pretending that she wasn't there.
She hid behind her orange chair.
But all the witches knew.
She knew they knew.
What could she do?

"Fly Ernestine!" they would exclaim.
But every time it was the same.
She toppled off her broom in shame.
Her head was full of lumps.
All lumps and bumps
and broomstick-thumps.

She heard them talk behind her back.
"That witch flies like a maniac."
"She'd fall out of a Pontiac."
"She couldn't ride a sled."
Not Santa's sled!
Her face was red.

Still, Ernestine dreamed of the day
when she could fly her broom away.
And every Halloween they'd say,
"Let's ride with Ernestine."
Dream Ernestine.
The flying queen.

So Ernestine had never been
out on her broom on Halloween.
But witches everywhere were keen
to fly out on this night.
Tonight's the night.
A fright delight.

Her witchy friends said their good-byes,
as flying broomsticks filled the skies.
But Ernestine made spider pies,
and stayed home with her cat.
A cat named Splaaat.
Imagine that!

"I wish that I could go," she said.
"But I keep falling on my head.
A klutz like me should stay in bed,
till after Halloween."
No Halloween.
Poor Ernestine.

But then she made a witches' brew,
and stirred the pot and thought it through.
"A sled!" she said. "That's what I'll do.
I'll make myself a seat!"
A flying seat.
To trick or treat.

She took two broomsticks as a pair
and tied them underneath her chair.
She said, "I've got no time to spare,"
and sat down for her ride.
A chair to ride.
So soft and wide.

Now Ernestine had quite a night.
Her broomstick-chair kept her upright.
She gave her witchy friends a fright.
They whispered, "Where's her broom?"
No bumpy broom?
It made them fume!

The witches' council met at dawn.
They heard how Ernestine had gone.
"Oh, how she flew and carried on!"
"With brooms strapped to her chair!"
A flying chair.
Was that so rare?

"This simply can't be done," they cried.
"She must obey *The Witches' Guide*."
"We broomstick riders have our pride."
"This nonsense just won't do!"
What could they do?
Try something new?

Then Ernestine came in the room.
They said, "You're sorry, we presume."
"You know a witch should ride a broom."
"How dare you ride a chair!"
Her chair was there.
It wasn't fair.

The witches' council then decreed
to punish this unwitchly deed.
"Who knows where this new ride will lead?"
"What's next—a flying couch?"
Why not a couch?
Gee—what a grouch!

But Ernestine smiled at them all
and stood up straight and rather tall.
She said, "I really had a ball.
I loved my Halloween."
First Halloween
for Ernestine.

"I rode all night and knocked on doors
and buzzed some tricksters soaping stores.
While all of you got saddle sores,
I had a cushy ride."
No broom to ride.
No sore backside.

Then Ernestine, the flying queen,
said, "At the risk of sounding mean—
you're in a rut. Change your routine.
Relax and fly like me."
Oh, mercy me!
Did they agree?

She saw the council elders swoon.
Some witches joined her chair platoon.
Their shadows crossed the harvest moon
to test-drive a new ride.
They tried the ride.
Did they decide?

When next All Hallows' Eve came by,
their chairs and couches filled the sky.
The witches cheered, "It's time to fly!"
"Let's ride with Ernestine."
Go Ernestine!
It's Halloween.

An Interview with Witch Ernestine

1. How did Halloween get started?

Ernestine: Halloween used to be known as "All Hallows' Eve." It started in Ireland over two thousand years ago. It was a holiday to honor the dead. Halloween was all so serious back then. Now it's all about having fun. You get to celebrate with scary costumes and candy. I get to buzz you in my nifty flying broomstick-chair.

2. Did they trick or treat back then too?

Ernestine: They sure did. People would go from house to house, demanding food for the town feast. In England they asked for little cakes—and they had to ask for them in rhyme. Of course pranks and mischief were part of the celebrations back then too. We witches have always liked to play tricks. But those spooky ghosts are the worst.

3. Is Halloween still a big holiday?

Ernestine: Next to Christmas, Halloween is the biggest holiday all year. It's a really big deal with all the costumes, decorations, parties and pumpkins. And of course it's the sweetest holiday of all. There's always tons of wickedly delicious candy. I think orange is such an important color, don't you?

4. Why do we wear costumes on Halloween?

Ernestine: A long time ago, people wore animal heads and skins on Halloween. They did this to ward off evil spirits on this night of the dead. So over the years, everyone kept up the tradition by wearing costumes and masks. Play it safe. Make sure you can see clearly through your masks. Always carry a flashlight to keep those creepy zombies away too.

5. What were you stirring in your witches' brew?

Ernestine: We witches love to make big bubbling cauldrons of stew. Some witches use really weird stuff, like eye of newt and tongue of dog. But I was making my own yummy brew. My secret recipe calls for pumpkin-slime, gourds and grime, and one very seasoned scarecrow. Splaaat likes it when I add a can of spicy cackle-juice. Try it. You might like it too.

6. What kind of name is Splaaat for a cat?

Ernestine: Poor thing, he was a stray. He liked to jump on my broom when I was trying to fly. When I'd tumble off, he'd fall too and we'd both go *Splaaat* on the ground. So that's why I called him Splaaat. When he got older, he didn't like to fall so much. So he stayed home and ate spider pies and got fat. Now he rides with me in my broomstick-chair.

7. What's your favorite thing about Halloween?

Ernestine: I love all the ghoulishly grinning jack-o'-lanterns. Way back in the olden days, pumpkins weren't used to make jack-o'-lanterns. Jack-o'-lanterns were carved out of turnips, gourds and potatoes. Today some people grow pumpkins as big as Volkswagens. They win big prizes too.

8. Do you have any last minute Halloween suggestions?

Ernestine: Just dress up and have a howling good time! But remember: never ever go into strange houses. And don't eat your treats before your parents have looked at them. Do like me—travel in groups with your friends.

P.S. The scuttlebutt around the cauldron is that those snobby vampires think Halloween is tacky. So they're not going out this year. But I'll see you there—in my chair.

Trouble·Spots

Sometimes I think it's just not right,
when spots come that I don't invite!

Like when a wart grows on my hand.
Well, that's a bump I never planned.

And why do freckles like my nose?
Why don't they hide out on my toes?

My cuts and scrapes are hard to scratch.
The itch gets stuck beneath the patch.

I don't like pimples on my chin.
They feel like spotlights on my skin.

My chickenpox caused a commotion.
I smeared myself with creamy lotion.

But sometimes trouble spots don't last.
They come and leave me just as fast.

An ointment healed my wart at night.
And soon it disappeared from sight.

Some crusty scabs fell off my shin.
And left behind a brand-new skin.

My chickenpox came to an end.
But first they jumped on my best friend.

Now pimples—I'm confused about.
My zits keep popping in and out.

And freckles—I guess they're okay,
They really don't get in my way.

But some spots seem to stick like glue.
Most times there's nothing I can do.

So if they visit me this year,
I'll just ignore them in my mirror.

The Spot Report

1. Toads get a bad rap.

Contrary to popular wart-lore, you can't get warts from touching toads. You get warts after catching a certain virus. And warts are contagious. For example, if you touch a towel or a pencil that someone with a wart has used—you can get a wart too. Kids who bite their fingernails get warts more than kids who don't. So you can kiss a toad, but don't bite your nails.

2. Fair freckled friends.

Some kids start getting freckles at about five years old. These speckled spots are most common in kids with blond or red hair and blue eyes. Freckles are perfectly normal. Some kids don't like having them. There's no magic spot-remover to erase them. So flaunt your sun-kissed freckles and be happy.

3. Mirror, mirror, I've got zits.

Your skin has many tiny holes called pores. Sometimes oil and bacteria clog up those pores and create pimples. Everyone gets them, but nobody wants them. The first thing to do is—step away from the mirror and stop picking! Popping your zits will only make them worse. So grin and bear them. They mean you're growing up.

4. Scabs stick together.

When you cut yourself, a magical thing happens. Special donut-shaped blood cells, called platelets, spring into action. They stick together like glue to stop the bleeding. Then they form a scab around the area to protect it. It's very tempting to pick at the scab. Don't do it. You'll just rip the skin and undo all the good work. Your scab will thank you by falling off when it's good and ready.

5. Yikes! It's the pox!

Chickenpox is caused by a virus. Kids with chickenpox are very contagious. And the spots sure are itchy. It's hard not to scratch something that's driving you crazy. But scratching can tear your skin and leave scars. Sometimes an oatmeal bath can help to relieve the itch. Yes, oatmeal—the breakfast cereal of chickenpox champions.

Mrs. Magilvery's Silvery Shawl

"She's wearing her shawl again," children would say,
when Mrs. Magilvery went out each day.
The kids were so curious, but who wouldn't be?
They wanted to know why she wore it, you see.

"Oh, Mrs. Magilvery," she heard them call,
"why are you wearing your silvery shawl?"
"You just never know," Mrs. M answered back
and hurried away with a *clickety-clack*.

Then Mrs. Magilvery met Mary-Lou.
She cried, "Mrs. M, I don't know what to do.
My wagon is broken," she said teary-eyed.
"I wanted to take Kitty out for a ride.

"But just as I started to tow her around,
the handle broke off, and it fell to the ground."
Then Mrs. Magilvery said, "I can see.
Your handle is broken as broken can be."

She took off her shawl. "You can fix it," she said.
"Try tying my shawl for a handle instead."
So Mary-Lou's cat got her ride after all.
Thanks to Mrs. Magilvery's silvery shawl.

The very next day, Mrs. M took a walk.
Her silvery shawl was tied over her frock.
Then down near the pond, she met Wee Willy Witt.
He was kicking and screaming and throwing a fit.

"Today of all days," she heard Wee Willy wail,
"I can't join the race with a hole in my sail!"
Then Mrs. Magilvery said, "I can see.
Your sail has a hole in it, big as can be.

"Try rigging my shawl like a sail to your mast.
Then as the wind blows it, your boat will go fast."
So Wee Willie Witt won the race with his yawl.
Thanks to Mrs. Magilvery's silvery shawl.

Now on her way home, she met gadabout Gert
who looked all upset like her feelings were hurt.
Gert said, "Mrs. M—it's our masquerade dance.
I wish I could go, but I haven't a chance.

"My friends are all ready, but I'll have to miss.
I don't have a costume—I can't go like this!"
Then Mrs. Magilvery said, "I can see.
You certainly need to dress up. I agree.

"Try wearing my silvery shawl like a cape.
Then make a tiara with cardboard and tape."
So gadabout Gert got to go to the ball,
Thanks to Mrs. Magilvery's silvery shawl.

And so this was how Mrs. M spent her days.
She lent out her shawl—oh, in so many ways.
It made a small hammock. It made a big kite.
It made a warm scarf on a cold winter's night.

They used it at picnics to spread on the grass.
On "Show-and-Tell" days, the kids brought it to class.
It worked as a kerchief to hide a bad "do."
And once on a full moon, the stork used it too.

She wasn't surprised when the kids came to call.
They said, "Mrs. M, now we'd *all* like a shawl.
You just never know when you need one, you see.
They're always as handy as handy can be."

Then Mrs. Magilvery said, "Oh, I know.
I have some material. Come in and sew."
So gadabout Gert picked a fabric in blue.
And Mary-Lou said, "I want silver like you."

"You girls can make girl-shawls," Wee Willie Witt said.
"But I'll make a pirate's bandana instead."
Then everyone measured and cut out a square.
While Mrs. M coached from her favorite chair.

And when the kids finished, they jumped up with glee.

They wore their creations for others to see.

Now everyone's happy and having a ball,

thanks to Mrs. Magilvery's silvery shawl.

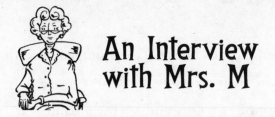

An Interview with Mrs. M

1. When did you start wearing your shawl every day?

Mrs. Magilvery: It all started a long time ago. One day I wore it because it was chilly outside. Later that day it rained, and I used it to cover my head. Then when the sun came out, I put it on the grass and had a picnic. From then on, I wore it every day—just in case.

2. What kind of boat is a yawl?

Mrs. Magilvery: A yawl is a sailboat with two masts. One tall mast holds a big sail, and one shorter mast holds a small sail. Wee Willy Witt had a hole in the big sail. We replaced the sail with my shawl, and he won the race. Will said the flapping fringe made the sailboat go extra fast.

3. How can we make a shawl like yours?

Mrs. Magilvery: It's easy. You could use an old sheet or tablecloth as your material. Make sure you get permission first. Just follow these simple steps and have fun!

A. Cut a large square piece of material. It should measure about as tall as you are on all four sides.

B. Decorate with buttons, beads, glitter glue, marker or anything you like.

C. Add trim by sewing fringe all around the edges. Or you could put a tassel on each of the four corners.

4. How did Wee Willy Witt make a pirate's bandana?

Mrs. Magilvery: That was easy too. He just followed steps A and B above. Willy made his square a little smaller than the girls' and he didn't add any fringe. Next he folded it into a triangle. Then he tied it on his head backward like a pirate. Try it. You'll look just like Captain Hook.

5. What's the funniest thing anyone has ever done with your shawl?

Mrs. Magilvery: Well, one time gadabout Gert had a big rip in the seat of her jeans. All the kids could see her underwear! She tied my silvery shawl around her waist to hide the hole in her pants. She and her friends giggled all the way home.

6. What's the coolest thing anyone's ever done with it?

Mrs. Magilvery: Once, Mary-Lou's poor little kitten fell into a well. Mary-Lou dangled my shawl down the hole. Kitty grabbed the soft silvery material and hung on with her claws. Then Mary-Lou pulled the shawl up out of the well, kitten and all. That was the best!

7. Is your silvery shawl magic?

Mrs. Magilvery: I don't think my shawl is magic. But then again, it can be used in so many ways, you just never know. Sometimes when we use our imaginations, simple things can become whatever we want them to be.

Big Blue Funk

I've fallen in a big blue funk.
I'm not sure how far down I've sunk.
And as I write I wonder why,
I'm feeling sad and want to cry.

I wish that I was glad inside.
I'd ride my bike or swing and slide.
But I don't feel like going out,
so I'll stay in my room and pout.

I wish I knew why I'm so blue.
I wish I knew what I could do.
I wish I knew what I could say
to make this feeling go away.

My pen is running out of ink.
It's very difficult to think.
A rhyming poem is hard to write
when words are hiding out of sight.

My inside voice is shouting out!
I'm not sure what it's all about.
But every line I write in rhyme
makes me feel better all the time.

And soon I'm smiling through my frown.
My poem has turned me upside-down.
The more I write the more I see
that being sad is part of me.

I'm ready now to go outside.
And take my bike out for a ride.
I'll grab my mitt and play some ball,
but first I'll give my friends a call.

That big blue funk sure made me blue.
But next time, I'll know what to do.
I'll get some paper and a pen
and write till I feel glad again.

Blues News

Everyone gets into a big blue funk for all kinds of reasons. It's okay to feel like a sad sack once in a while. But finding ways to give those blues a good boot can be fun. Keep reading for some ideas that might work for you.

1. Take the lid off.

Write, draw, cry, talk or go for a walk. Do something to let it out. The big blue funk likes to live in places that are all sealed up. So write down your thoughts. Or talk about your feelings with someone you love, like your parents or best friend. Soon "old blue" will disappear into the wild blue yonder.

2. What's bugging you?

Maybe you don't know why you're feeling blue. That means you might have to think about a lot of stuff to figure it out. So turn off the TV and sit quietly with your thinking cap on. Pets make great pals when you noodle on your problems. The best way to find the answer is to take the lid off.

3. It's time to rhyme.

Try reading a favorite rhyming story or poem. It's a scientific fact that you can't be grumpy and read a rhyme at the same time. (Well, maybe not scientific, but it works.) And what about singing or rapping a rhyme to your own tune? You can't cry the blues when you're singing to a funky-monkey beat.

4. Write on!

Go for it. Write your own stories and poems. Writing is like word-medicine that makes you feel better. It helps you to listen from the inside out. Did you know there are no words that rhyme with month, orange, silver and purple?

5. Shake on it.

Sometimes you can shake the blues right out of your body. Try running, biking, swimming, playing soccer or baseball when you're feeling down. That big blue funk hates being disturbed. So get some exercise to shake it up and shake it out.

Pat Skene has no strange pets or weird habits like some of her characters do; however, she does have eleven rocking chairs and two outdoor swings. Could that be where she gets her wonderful sense of rhythm? Pat lives with her husband in Cobourg, Ontario.